Skill Sharpeners

Kindergarten

Math

Activity Book

W9-CYA-825

Silver Dolphin

San Diego, California

Table of Contents

Shapes on the Farm

Color the squares ■ brown. Color the rectangles ▬ red.
Color the triangles ▲ black. Color the circles ○ yellow.
Color the hexagons ⬡ green.

Farm Shapes

Circle all the cylinders. Trace all the spheres.
Put an "X" on all the cubes. Put a check ✓ on all the cones.

Cube Cone Cylinder Sphere

Shape Up

Use your blocks to match the shapes and create the pictures. Then remove the blocks and color the shapes to match the block colors.

Farm Fun

Write the correct words on the lines.

The bird is _____ the tree.

| beside   in |

The dog is _____ the doghouse.

| in front of   above |

The rooster is _____ the barn.

| above   behind |

The eggs are _____ the bird.

below   on

The pig is _____ the mud.

below   next to

The horse is _____ the barn.

behind   below

Animals on the Farm

How many of each animal can you see?
Write the number on the line.

Horses _____   Sheep _____

Cows _____   Pigs _____

Hens _____   Cats _____

Dogs _____   Crows _____

Look at All the Animals

Count the animals and write the number.

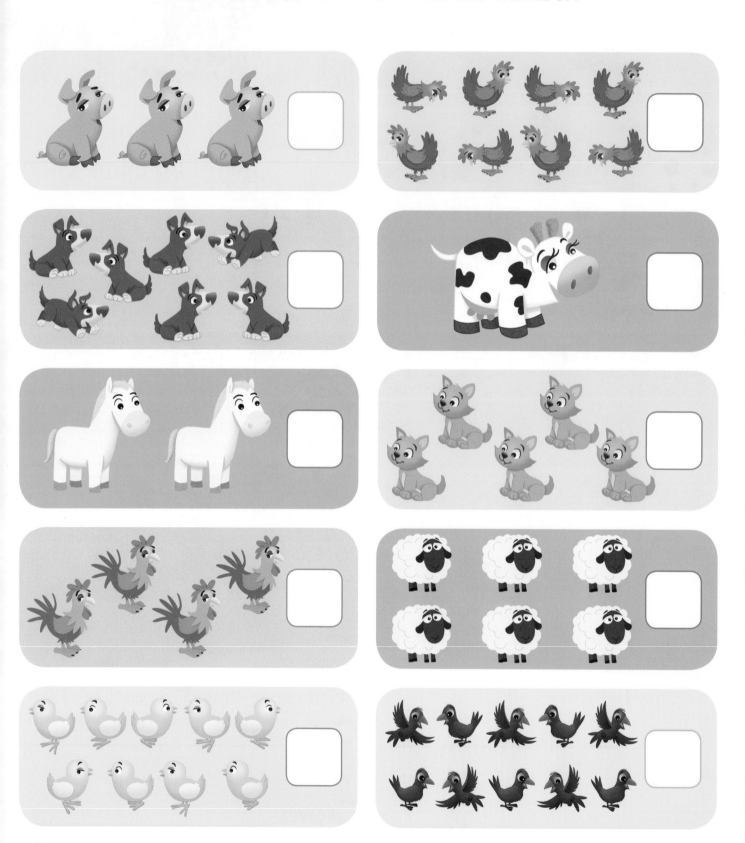

Animal Row

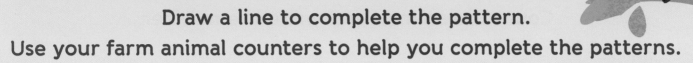

Draw a line to complete the pattern.
Use your farm animal counters to help you complete the patterns.

| red horse | yellow cow | red horse | yellow cow | red horse | _____ | yellow cow |
| | | | | | | red horse |

| blue pig | blue pig | green sheep | green sheep | blue pig | _____ | blue pig |
| | | | | | | green sheep |

green horse	yellow sheep	red pig	green horse	yellow sheep	_____	green horse
						red pig
						yellow sheep

blue cow	red pig	green sheep	blue cow	red pig	_____	blue cow
						red pig
						green sheep

Make your own animal pattern.

_____   _____   _____   _____   _____   _____

11

Everything Counts

Count the animals and write the number.

How many eggs did the hen lay? ☐

How many ears of corn are in the row? ☐

How many crows are on the scarecrow? ☐

How many dogs are under the tree?

How many pigs are eating?

How many horses are going for a walk?

Dogs, Birds, and Eggs, Oh My!

Match the number to the pictures
(eggs, dogs, birds, cornstalks, hay bales).

16 _____   17 _____   18 _____

19 _____   20 _____

On the Farm

Count and write the number in each group.
Circle the group with more.

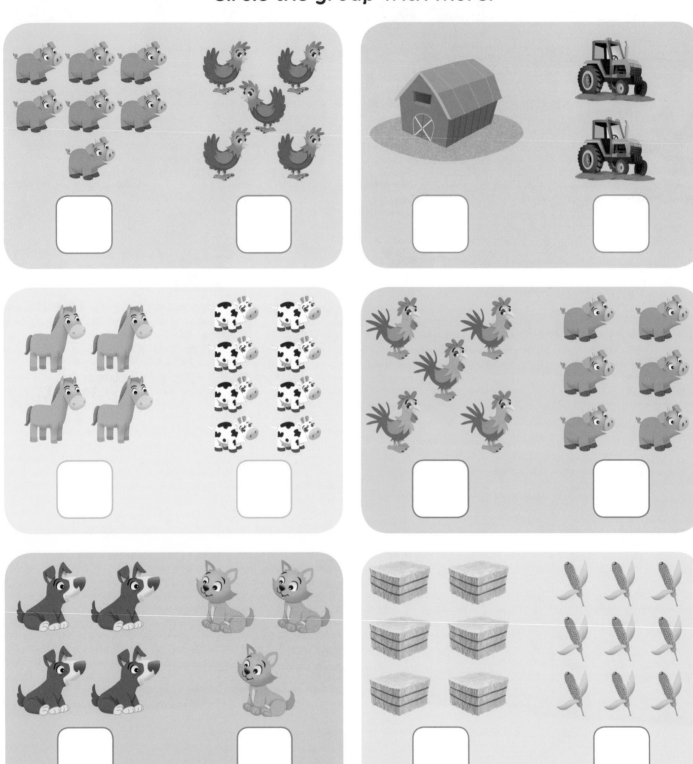

Farmer's Count

Count and write the number in each group.
Circle the group with less.

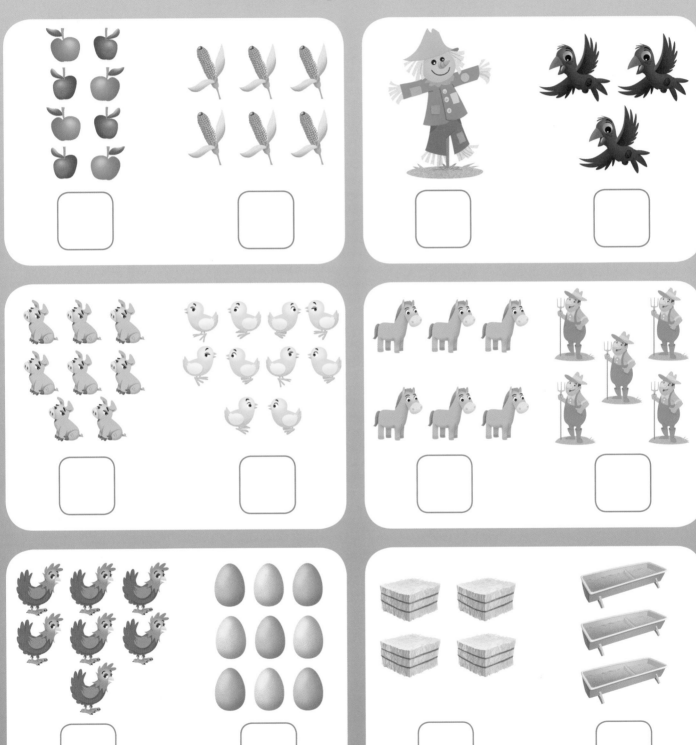

The More We Get Together

Draw a line to connect a picture from one group to a picture in the other group. Then circle the group that has more.

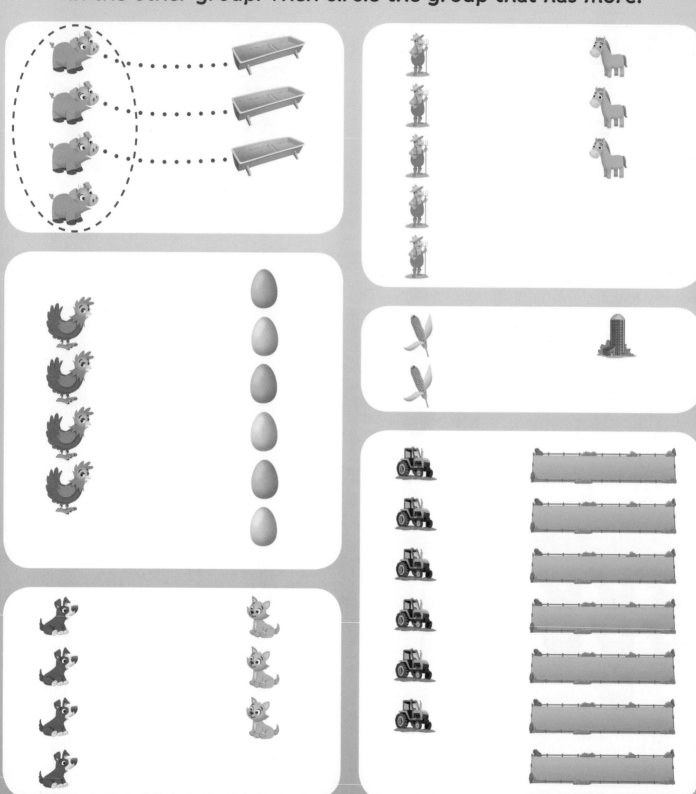

Farmer Brown's Animals

Count the animals to find the answer.

+ = __3__ horses

+ = ____ pigs

+ = ____ hens

+ = ____ cows

+ = ____ sheep

+ = ____ roosters

Fill the Field

Use your farm animals to help find the missing numbers.

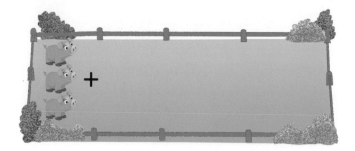

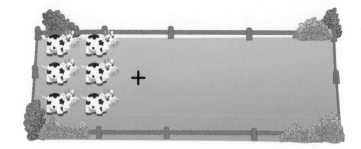

____3____ + ____5____ = ____8____   ____6____ + _____ = ____10____

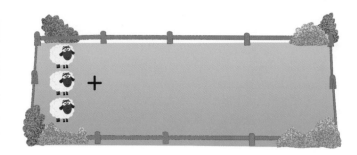

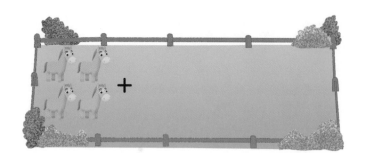

____3____ + _____ = ____7____   ____4____ + _____ = ____9____

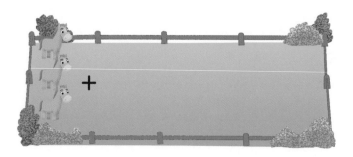

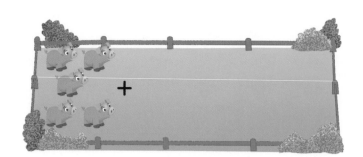

____3____ + _____ = ____4____   ____5____ + _____ = ____6____

20

Here We Come

Use the pictures to help write the addition sentence.

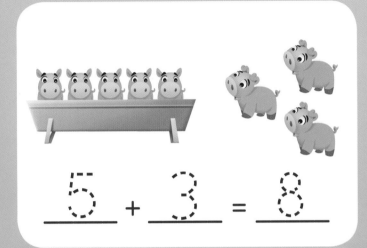

$$5 + 3 = 8$$

_____ + _____ = _____

_____ + _____ = _____

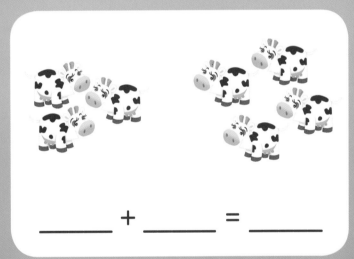

_____ + _____ = _____

_____ + _____ = _____

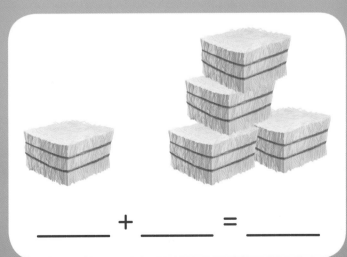

_____ + _____ = _____

Fill Them Up

Add the numbers. Use the animal counters if you need help.

$4 + 1 =$ _____

$2 + 3 =$ _____

$5 + 5 =$ _____

$0 + 7 =$ _____

$3 + 6 =$ _____

$7 + 1 =$ _____

$10 + 0 =$ _____ $6 + 2 =$ _____

$1 + 5 =$ _____ $1 + 1 =$ _____

$8 + 1 =$ _____ $9 + 0 =$ _____

$3 + 2 =$ _____ $1 + 3 =$ _____

Animals, Animals Everywhere

Add your animal counters to the pictures.
Then complete the addition sentences.

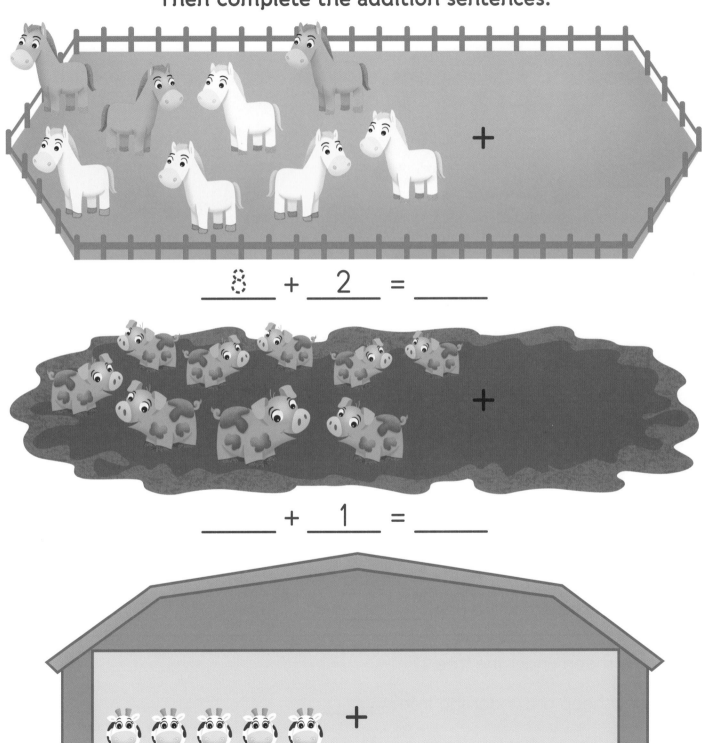

_8_ + _2_ = _____

_____ + _1_ = _____

_____ + _2_ = _____

Farmer Brown Adds On

Put 1 more pig in the mud.

How many pigs are in the mud? _____

Put 1 more horse in the pen.

How many horses are in the pen? _____

Put 1 more sheep under the tree.

How many sheep are under the tree? _____

Put 1 more cow in front of the barn.

How many cows are in front of the barn? _____

Write the number of animals
in the second pen, then add.

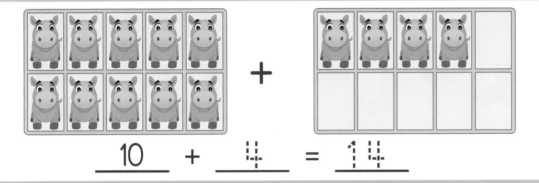

_____10_____ + _____4_____ = _____14_____

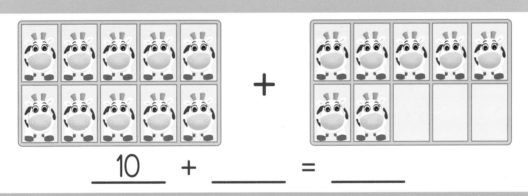

_____10_____ + _____ = _____

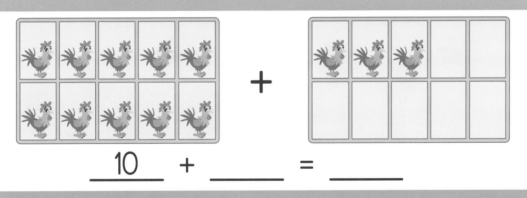

_____10_____ + _____ = _____

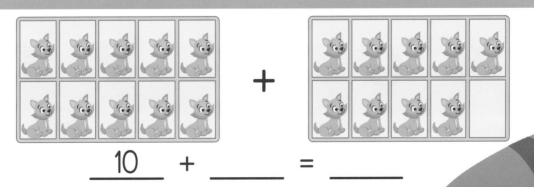

_____10_____ + _____ = _____

Animal Roundup

Circle a group of 10 animals, then write
an addition sentence to show how many there are in total.

$$10 + 8 = 18$$

_____ + _____ = _____

_____ + _____ = _____

_____ + _____ = _____

Measure Up

Circle the taller cornstalk.

Circle the shorter animal.

Circle the longer fence.

Circle the shorter tractor.

Circle the larger object.

Circle the smaller object.

How Many Are Left?

Cross out, then complete the problems.

3 - 1 = __2__

8 - 5 = ____

2 - 0 = ____

9 - 6 = ____

10 - 2 = ____

4 - 4 = ____

Write the number problem below the picture.

There are 5 hay bales in the barn. Farmer Brown takes 2 away on the tractor. How many are left?

$5 - 2 = 3$

The chicken laid 4 eggs in the nest. The farmer took 4 away in his basket. How many are left?

_____ - _____ = _____

There are 3 horses in the field. The farmer rides 1 horse into town. How many are left in the field?

_____ - _____ = _____

4 cornstalks are standing in the field. The farmer loads 3 onto the truck. How many are left in the field?

_____ - _____ = _____

There are 6 dogs on the porch. 4 dogs run away. How many are left on the porch?

_____ - _____ = _____

There is 1 bird on the scarecrow. 1 flies away. How many are left?

_____ - _____ = _____

Barnyard Subtraction

Use the animal counters to help you subtract
and find the answers to the problems.

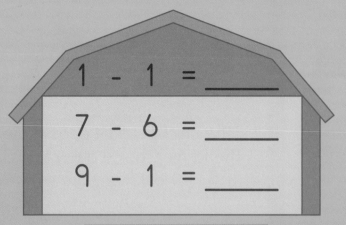

1 - 1 = _____

7 - 6 = _____

9 - 1 = _____

10 - 1 = _____

8 - 2 = _____

3 - 2 = _____

6 - 3 = _____

4 - 0 = _____

5 - 1 = _____

2 - 2 = _____

7 - 2 = _____

4 - 2 = _____